FRANKLIN PARK PUBLIC LIBRARY

FRANKLIN PARK, ILL.

Each borrower is held responsible for all library material drawn on his card and for fines accruing on the same. No material will be issued until such fine has been paid.

All injuries to library material beyond reasonable wear and all losses shall be made good to the satisfaction of the Librarian.

THE INCREDIBLE
Journey to the
BEGINNING OF TIME

Published by
Peter Bedrick Books
156 Fifth Avenue
New York, NY 1010

Library of Congress Cataloging-in-Publication Data

Harris, Nicholas, 1956-
    The incredible journey to the beginning of time / Nicholas Harris
; [illustrations, Alessandro Rabatti, Andrea Ricciardi di Gaudesi].
-- 1st US ed.
        p. cm.
    Includes index.
    Summary: Presents a geological, biological, and social history of
the earth by focussing on the same four locales--New York,
southwestern France, the Nile Valley, and northern China--through
thirteen time periods covering more than 550 million years.
    ISBN 0-87226-293-6
    1. Historical geology--Juvenile literature. 2. Civilization-
-Juvenile literature. [1. Historical geology. 2. Evolution.
3. Civilization.] I. Rabatti, Alessandro, ill. II. Ricciardi,
Andrea, ill. III. Title.
QE28.3.H37 1998
900--dc21

                                                          98-18896
                                                          CIP
                                                          AC

Created and produced by Orpheus Books Ltd

Text and design
Nicholas Harris

Research and text contributor
Dr Robert Peberdy

Illustrations
Alessandro Rabatti, Andrea Ricciardi di Gaudesi

Consultants
Dr Andrew Sherratt, Senior Assistant Keeper, Department of Antiquities,
Ashmolean Museum, University of Oxford
Dr Owen White, Lecturer in Modern History, Merton College,
University of Oxford
Dr Michael Benton, Reader in Palaeontology, University of Bristol
Iain Nicolson, Visiting Fellow, University of Hertfordshire

Production
Joanna Turner

Printed and bound in Singapore

First US edition, 1998

05 04 03 02 01 00 99 1 2 3 4 5

THE INCREDIBLE
Journey to the
BEGINNING OF TIME

Nicholas Harris

THIS BOOK is like a time machine. Starting from now, you are about to travel back through time. Occasionally, the clock stops and you can take a look at what the world was like at a particular date in the past. To begin with, your journey takes you back hundreds of years—back through the Victorian times, the Middle Ages, the time of the Romans, to the dawn of civilization. Later on, you start to make hops of thousands of years—back through the early years of humans themselves—then giant leaps of *millions* of years to the Age of Dinosaurs, to a time when there was no life on land at all...to the first days of the Earth itself.

Your time machine has four windows. Through them, you can watch the ages rolling back in four very different places around the world: New York City, south-western France, the Nile Valley in Egypt and northern China. For each, the viewpoint is always the same but, as you will see, the scenery changes dramatically from one date to the next...

PETER BEDRICK BOOKS
NEW YORK

THE WORLD TODAY

• The world's human population is almost 6,000 million, of whom about one-fifth live in China. The largest urban area is Tokyo, Japan, with about 27 million inhabitants. World population is growing by about 236,000 a day.

• The tallest building in the world is the 1483 feet Petronas Centre in Kuala Lumpur, Malaysia.

• The fastest means of travel from Europe to America is by *Concorde* jet. The journey takes about three-and-a-half hours.

• People have reached the Poles (North 1909, South 1911), discovered penicillin (1928), split the atom (1932), exploded an atom bomb (1945), landed on the Moon (1969), sent a space probe to view the planets (1975-1989) and wiped out smallpox (1977).

"The electric sign turns to WALK, and people milling on the sidewalk surge forward across the road. Young men on rollerblades zip through the throng of office workers and women with children and shopping. There are people representing ethnic groups from all over the world: blacks, Europeans, Hispanics, Chinese, Asians and many others. The snarling traffic revs up in anticipation of reclaiming the streets once more."

NEW YORK USA

4

Ｎ EW YORK is the largest city in the world's most powerful country, the USA. The business district of Manhattan is always crowded with people, cars, buses and taxis. Millions of people travel into the city every day to work in the offices. Skyscrapers like the World Trade Center have replaced some older buildings. A vast network of subways (underground railways) has been tunnelled beneath the city streets.

Ｗ ESTERN EUROPE is one of the richest parts of the world. Even the countryside, once the home of poor peasants, is prosperous. Modern machinery has replaced the need for farm labourers. Many people living in villages now travel to work in cities by car or train, or work in local businesses or shops, or at home. Their houses contain televisions, videos and CD players, and are mostly comfortably furnished.

Ｅ GYPT'S POPULATION has risen from 9 million in 1900 to more than 57 million today. Egypt is quite a poor country, chiefly dependent on tourism. Visitors from all over the world flock there to see the pyramids and the temples of Thebes, to take a cruise on the Nile and to shop in the bazaars. Half the Egyptian population still live in the countryside.

Ｃ HINA has been in turmoil in the twentieth century. After centuries of imperial rule, the last emperor was overthrown in 1911. The Communist Party took over government in 1949. Three-quarters of China's vast population still live by farming. But modern ways of life are slowly appearing. The mining of coal, formed millions of years ago, is an important industry.

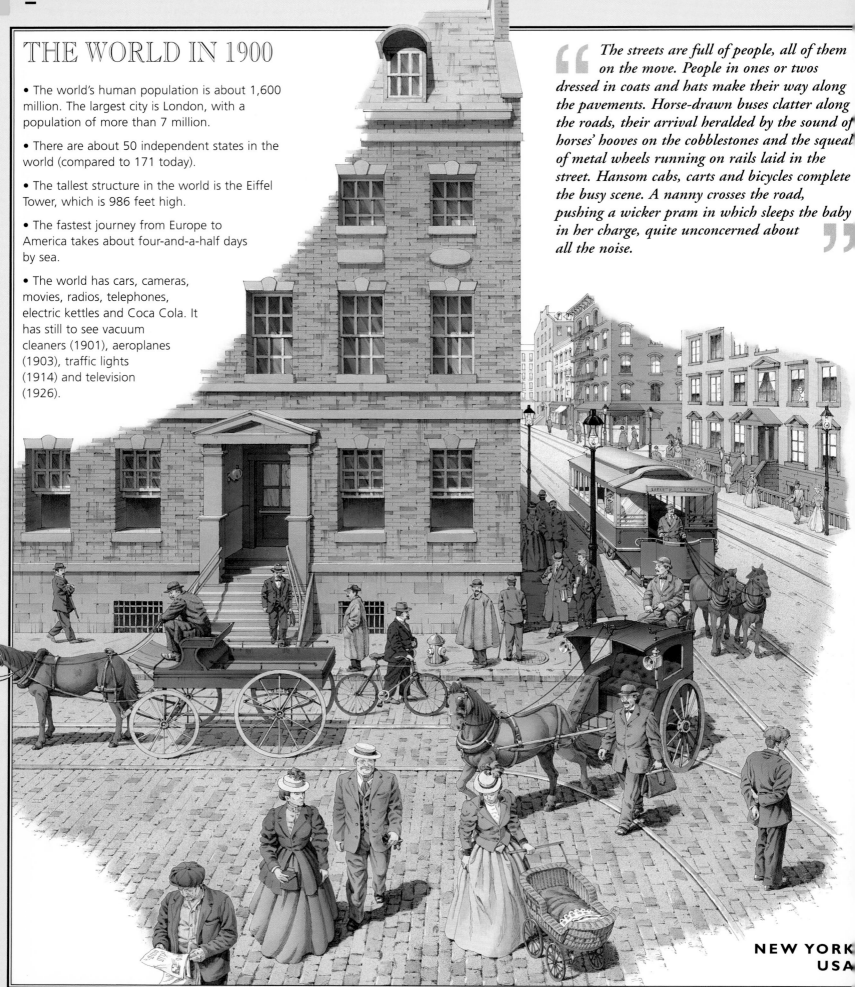

THE WORLD IN 1900

- The world's human population is about 1,600 million. The largest city is London, with a population of more than 7 million.

- There are about 50 independent states in the world (compared to 171 today).

- The tallest structure in the world is the Eiffel Tower, which is 986 feet high.

- The fastest journey from Europe to America takes about four-and-a-half days by sea.

- The world has cars, cameras, movies, radios, telephones, electric kettles and Coca Cola. It has still to see vacuum cleaners (1901), aeroplanes (1903), traffic lights (1914) and television (1926).

" *The streets are full of people, all of them on the move. People in ones or twos dressed in coats and hats make their way along the pavements. Horse-drawn buses clatter along the roads, their arrival heralded by the sound of horses' hooves on the cobblestones and the squeal of metal wheels running on rails laid in the street. Hansom cabs, carts and bicycles complete the busy scene. A nanny crosses the road, pushing a wicker pram in which sleeps the baby in her charge, quite unconcerned about all the noise.* "

NEW YORK USA

NEW YORK is a bustling city. Much of Manhattan island has been built over—even its shoreline has been extended by landfill. Wealthy people live in this part of town. They have large houses and servants, and they travel by horse-drawn cab. Ships arrive at New York's busy port from all parts of the world carrying both goods and people. Immigrants have come to the United States hoping to make a new and better life.

FACTORIES have sprung up all over Europe. Manufactured goods start to appear in villages and towns everywhere. Farmers use longer-lasting metal tools and machines in the fields, while people can travel from village to village by bicycle. Long-distance journeys are made by steam train. The railways make it possible for farmers to sell their produce in cities and for people to leave the countryside to find work there.

1900

EGYPT, like most of Africa, is under the rule of a European power. In Egypt's case, it is Britain. European faces mingle with those of Egyptians in the crowded bazaar. Egypt is a major trading station and goods turn up here from all over Africa and Asia. More or less anything is for sale in the street: carpets, clothes, cloth, spices, pots and pans, animals.

CHINA has been under the rule of the Manchu Emperors for more than 250 years. Its once-vast empire has collapsed, it has been defeated in several wars and it has lost the prosperity it used to enjoy. Life is hard for the peasants. The population has increased, so the amount of land held by each person has become smaller. Transport of goods is mostly by camels or mules.

THE WORLD IN 1650

• The world's human population is about 610 million. The largest city is Beijing in China, with a population of about 1 million.

• The world's tallest building is probably Notre Dame cathedral in Strasbourg, France, whose spire takes it to 463 feet high.

• Scientists are taking advantage of recent inventions: the compound microscope (c.1590), the telescope (1609), the thermometer (1592), the calculator (1623) and the barometer (1643).

• All the continents are known to Europeans except for Antarctica. New European settlements have sprung up in South and Central America, and on the eastern seaboard of North America. The African interior is largely unexplored. Dutch seamen have recently explored the coast of Australia.

• The journey from Europe to America takes about three months by sea.

The distinctive smells of freshly brewed tea, newly cut wood and farm animals mingle curiously in the village square. People gossip as they work or meet to discuss local goings-on. The hum of their conversation is accompanied by the clatter of the grinding mill being turned by two powerful oxen, and the whoops and squeals of children at play. Workers carrying heavy loads and some wealthier folk in flowing gowns make their way through the gathering.

NORTHERN CHINA

P EOPLE from the Netherlands have recently bought the island of Manhattan from the natives (for about $25) and founded their own settlement, called New Amsterdam, at the island's southern tip. It is a town of about 1000 people and 120 houses, many of them brick-built with steep roofs in the style of a typical Dutch town. The English navy will take over the settlement in 1664 and rename it New York.

I N THIS VILLAGE, the sheep are brought in from their hill pastures to have their fleeces sheared off. Merchants from larger towns buy the wool and sell it on to cloth manufacturers. The only means of travel is by horse, by horse-drawn carriage, or by foot. France has great agricultural wealth and a large population. Under King Louis XIV (still only 11 years old) it will become one of the world's most powerful nations.

E GYPT is now part of the powerful Ottoman empire and ruled from Istanbul in Turkey. The Ottoman emperors are determined to keep the country under control. They use highly trained soldiers called janissaries (from the Turkish word meaning "new force") to maintain their authority throughout the empire. They are seen here riding on camels.

A FTER 300 YEARS of rule by emperors of the Ming dynasty, the Chinese empire has been seized by outsiders from Manchuria, north-east of China itself. The population goes on increasing, and villages like this continue to prosper. While craftsmen work, others drink tea, which is now a popular drink throughout China. Ordinary people now wear cotton clothes.

1650

THE WORLD IN 1250

• The world's human population is about 360 million, of whom about 240 million (two-thirds) live in Asia.

• The largest city in the world is Hangzhou in southern China, with a population of approximately 1.5 million.

• Around this time, the Mongol Empire is at its height. The greatest land empire in history, it extends from Korea in the east to Poland in the west, taking in China, Russia, Central Asia and much of the Middle East.

• The Chinese have invented printing, paper money, the umbrella, matches, gunpowder, spinning machines and the magnetic compass—all hundreds of years before this date.

• European travellers have ventured into Asia and rounded the north-western coast of Africa. The Vikings, the most adventurous explorers, have crossed the Atlantic Ocean from Scandinavia and landed in Newfoundland (c. 1000).

The village is buzzing with excitement. It's the day of the annual fair, and people from all over the region are arriving with their wares. Horses and carts are loaded with sacks of grain, and people herding pigs, cattle and sheep throng the streets. People selling all kinds of goods mingle with the crowds, calling out to attract customers. Their shouts mingle with the general hubbub— people talking and arguing, children screaming and laughing, animals snorting and squealing—all this, and the joyful music of singers and fiddlers, too.

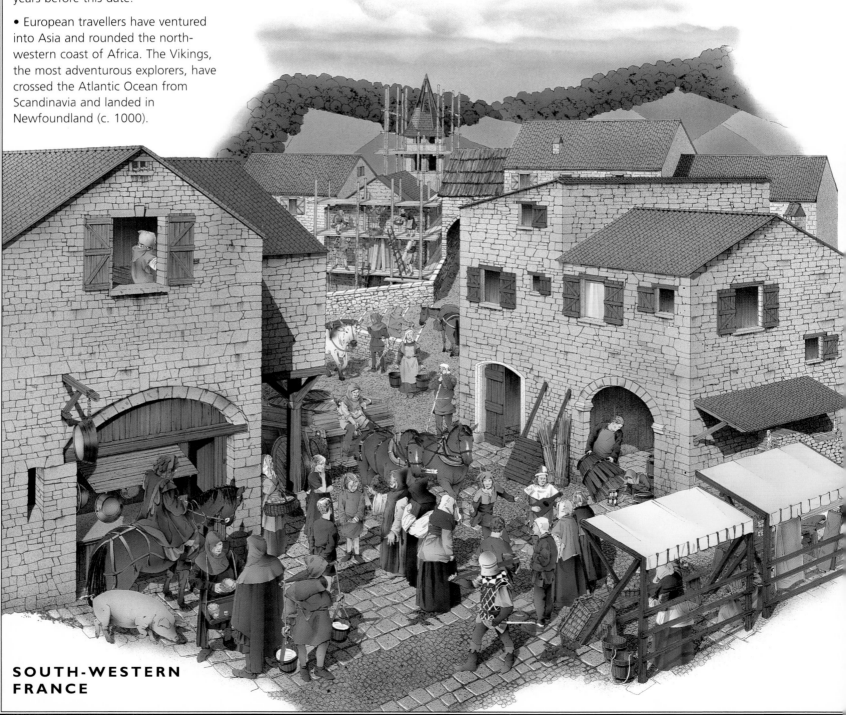

SOUTH-WESTERN FRANCE

THE NATIVES of Manhattan island live in wooden-framed, bark-covered houses. They hunt, fish and raise crops for their food. To defend their villages against enemy tribes, they have built palisades (strong fences) all round them. Every summer the chiefs from the villages meet for a conference, or "pow-wow". When chiefs die, their bones are kept in a special house surrounded by its own palisade.

AS IN MANY parts of Europe during the Middle Ages, south-western France is governed by wealthy landowners. The peasants farm the land and pay taxes to the lord. In recent years, the population has risen, so forests have been cut down to provide space for new villages and fields. The people have more produce to sell, so they flock to a fair with their animals or grain, hoping also to buy goods from travelling merchants.

ARABS conquered Egypt over 600 years ago. Since then, many of the inhabitants have become Muslims (followers of the teachings of the Prophet Muhammad). The people are a mixture of Egyptians and Arabs, and most speak Arabic. Their cities have stout walls and many mosques—places of Muslim worship—with tall towers, or minarets.

NORTHERN CHINA is now under the rule of the Mongols. Over the past few hundred years, China's population has grown considerably and become prosperous. Markets have sprung up in many places. People come to the village from other villages carrying their wares on wheelbarrows or in baskets. The market also attracts wandering entertainers.

THE WORLD IN AD 100

• The world's human population is about 180 million, of whom about 125 million (70%) live in Asia. The world's largest city is Rome (extensively damaged by fire in AD 64), with a population of about 1 million.

• There are four great empires in the world: the Roman in Europe, the Han in China, the Parthian in the Middle East, and the Kushan in northern India. Trade, mostly in silk, spices, glass, gold and silver, flows between them.

• The Roman empire is nearly at its height. It covers an area the size of Australia. The empire extends from Scotland to Egypt, and from Portugal to the eastern shores of the Black Sea.

• The next century will see the invention of paper (AD 105), the dome (AD 128) and the wheelbarrow (AD 200). Coins, carpets and clocks already exist.

" Ox-carts bearing hay arrive from the countryside and jostle for space in the busy streets along with soldiers, tradesmen and townspeople. The Roman soldiers, speaking to one another in a different language—Latin—from that used by the local inhabitants, wear shiny helmets and body armour, and carry large shields and swords. The houses, many with fine balconies and colonnades, have been skilfully built out of stone and wood and look as though they will last forever. Steps in the street enable people to cross from one side to another when the streets are flooded after heavy rain. "

AD 100

SOUTH-WESTERN FRANCE

NATIVE AMERICANS have settled on this sheltered coast. They no longer move from camp to camp, hunting whatever they can find. Instead, they live in sturdily built houses made of branches and animal skins, and have begun to grow their own food. Their main crop is maize, grown in the small fields around the settlement, but they continue to fish and to collect fruit and berries.

LIKE MUCH of Europe, south-western France has been conquered by the all-powerful Roman army and incorporated into the vast Roman empire. The Romans have built a network of new, straight roads across the continent. They have also constructed many new towns, complete with fine buildings and high stone walls. Besides government offices, there are houses, market stalls and baths, and perhaps also a theatre.

FOR THE LAST 130 years, Egypt, like France, has been part of the Roman empire. With its fertile lands along the Nile, Egypt is an important source of grain. Merchants ship the grain across the Mediterranean Sea and sell it in the markets of Rome. Ordinary Egyptians continue to live much as they have always done, relying on the Nile to water their fields every year.

FOR MOST of the last 300 years, China has been united in a vast empire ruled by a single emperor. The empire is very well organized. Government officials travel from place to place by chariot along specially built roads. The officials issue instructions about all kinds of matters, from which weights and measures may legally be used, to which crops may be grown.

THE WORLD IN 1500 BC

• The world's human population is about 30 million. The largest city is probably Ur in Mesopotamia, which has a population of 250,000.

• The tallest building in the world is the Great Pyramid at Giza, Egypt, erected about 1000 years earlier. It stands 480 feet high, and will hold the record for another 3000 years (despite the loss of 33 feet when its topmost stones fall off).

• People have settled most parts of the world, including the Arctic and the southernmost tip of South America. They will not reach New Zealand, however, for more than another 2000 years.

• The only people that can write—probably only a few thousand—live in the Middle East, Egypt, Turkey, China and on the Mediterranean island of Crete.

• Somewhere in the world, people are using pins, nails, mirrors, baths, bottles, spoons and balls.

Just a short distance away, there is nothing but vast expanses of desert. But here, close to this magnificent river, the land is bustling with life. There are trees, fields of cereals, white buildings clustered together in villages and magnificent monuments. Small boats made of reeds, and some quite large sailing ships, crowd the river. People are busy in the fields harvesting the crop, tending their livestock, at home making food, or at the river's edge catching fish. A man pours water from the river into a newly dug channel.

**NILE VALLEY,
EGYPT**

THIS PART of Manhattan island is a swampy forest. People live in small groups, setting up a camp for a few weeks before moving on. They eat what they can find in the forest or the rivers. Women gather berries and nuts, while men hunt deer with spears. They use spear-throwers to help them throw spears with more force. They fish using simple nets. Canoes made from hollowed-out tree trunks allow them to fish in deeper waters.

MOST people live in small villages. They grow wheat and keep livestock. All their needs—food, clothes, firewood—come from the land they work. They may have some spare crops which they can sell in exchange for precious metals. The villagers have few tools, but they do have light wooden ploughs to break up the soil and let air into it. With the help of oxen, they cut furrows in the soil in both directions.

EGYPT has been a kingdom for 1500 years. The kings, or pharaohs, have great wealth and have built palaces, pyramids and temples. Worship of the gods is a very important part of a pharaoh's life. The ordinary people farm the land on the fertile banks of the Nile, growing emmer wheat and barley, and raising livestock. They use a *shaduf* to raise water out of the river.

NORTHERN CHINA is a prosperous land. It is the time of the Shang dynasty. The king has an army and raises taxes from ordinary people. There are many fine craftsmen, who are particularly skilled at working the metal bronze. They make bronze cooking vessels and knives, as well as wooden chariots and beautiful objects from the semi-precious stone jade.

THE WORLD IN 5000 BC

• The world's human population is about 6 million. The largest settlements—villages in the Middle East—have populations of no more than 5000 people.

• At about this time, the Black Sea is created. The land basin is rapidly infilled by the rising waters of the Mediterranean Sea.

• People already have brushes, needles, combs, fishing nets and boats. They have yet to invent ploughs (c.4000 BC), wheels (c. 3500 BC) and writing (c. 3200 BC).

• Between 8000 and 6000 BC, the modern-day Sahara desert was an expanse of grassland with wooded uplands and freshwater lakes. By 5000 BC, the Sahara has become drier, but it is still possible for people to herd cattle here.

It is a busy day in the village. Construction of one of the new houses is almost complete. The clay walls have been built. Only the thatch—a roof of millet stalks and reeds—remains to be fastened to the top of the wooden frame. Meanwhile, people are chopping down trees to make more room for cropfields, and gathering in the precious harvest. Children greet the successful return of the hunters with their kill, a young wild boar. Their excited cheers mingle with the squeals and snuffles of pigs and the bleating of goats.

NORTHERN CHINA

5000 BC

IT IS ABOUT 5000 years since the ice cap that once completely obliterated this landscape melted away. The sea level is still low, as a great deal of water remains frozen elsewhere in extensive polar and mountain ice sheets. So, for the time being, all this area is land. People have arrived from farther south to live and hunt in the lush, dense woodlands. Mastodons, now extinct, once roamed here, but deer are still plentiful.

SOMEWHERE in south-western France, a group of people are building a small settlement. They cut down and burn trees to make a clearing, then dig a ditch all round for protection against wild animals. The houses are made of clay, branches and straw. The settlers plant wheat, which they use to make bread, and keep pigs, goats and sheep, which provide milk, meat, wool and skins. They make pots from baked clay, which they use for storage.

IN EGYPT, people have begun to keep livestock, grow crops and live in villages. Every summer, the Nile waters rise and flood the valley, leaving behind a thin layer of new, rich soil either side of the river. The climate in the Nile valley is cooler and wetter than it will be in modern times. Large animals, including elephants and giraffes, thrive in the lush landscape.

MUCH OF northern China is covered by loess, a soft yellow soil that is easy to dig and very fertile, so the people are able to grow plenty of food. Their main crops are millet, a kind of cereal they use to make bread, and hemp, from which they make clothes. At the centre of each village is a large pyramid-shaped hut where people meet to talk.

5000 BC

THE WORLD 20,000 years ago

• This time in the Earth's history falls in the Pleistocene Epoch. It is the time of the Ice Ages, a period of alternately cold and warm phases (interglacials). During the cold phases, up to one-third of the globe is covered by ice sheets.

• This is the coldest point of the most recent cold phase. So much water is frozen in the ice sheets that sea levels are 330 feet lower than they will be in modern times. The continents of Asia and North America, once separated by sea, are linked by dry land.

• The world's human population is probably about 4 million.

• People live in Africa, Asia, Europe—and now also in Australia, which was colonized from south-east Asia perhaps 45,000 years earlier. People probably live in the Americas, too.

• People have invented spears, knives, bows and arrows, and lamps (using animal fat).

• The largest land animal in the world is a kind of mammoth. It stands about 15 feet high, and has tusks more than 16 feet long.

A deafening, blood-chilling roar goes up. A massive woolly mammoth collapses in the snow. Men shriek and punch the air with triumph, then summon up their last reserves of energy to jab or fling their spears into the writhing creature's body. The mammoth's roars dwindle to dying moans. People rush from their hillside cave to witness the great event. At least two of the brave hunters have been injured, but for this clan there will be food for many days to come. A lynx is scared away by all the commotion, while a herd of musk oxen looks on warily.

SOUTH-WESTERN FRANCE

M OST of North America lies under a thick ice sheet—up to two miles thick in places—including, near its southernmost edge, the area that will one day become New York City. During the last 5000 years the ice has spread down from polar regions to the north. Soon, as the climate gradually warms, the ice will start to retreat northwards again to the Arctic Ocean and Greenland.

S OUTH-WESTERN France is a cold, bleak land. On the rare occasions when the snow melts, the ground is covered with grass and moss. People live mainly by hunting animals and fishing. In this scene, men rush to kill a woolly mammoth, bringing the beast down with a barrage of spears. On the walls deep inside caves, the people of this region paint wonderful pictures of the animals they hunt.

W ITH so much water trapped in ice sheets, the world's supply of water has dwindled. In tropical regions, far from the ice sheets, rain has become rarer and rivers run dry. Tropical rainforests have shrunk, and deserts have spread across large areas. The once-mighty River Nile is a sluggish stream, wandering across an arid landscape.

P EOPLE in northern China live in a land where summer never comes. Plants are very scarce, so people rely instead on hunting animals for their food. Fortunately, large beasts such as the woolly rhinoceros are abundant. Groups of people live together in simple huts made of branches and covered by animal hides weighted down with boulders.

20,000 years ago

THE WORLD 500,000 years ago

• The world is in the grip of the Ice Ages, but this date falls within one of the warm periods, or interglacials. The ice sheets have retreated to the Poles, and warm conditions prevail as far north as England.

• Modern humans (*Homo sapiens*) have probably not yet appeared. But there is an early kind of human alive. Known as *Homo erectus* ("upright human"), they may be the direct ancestors of *Homo sapiens*. *Homo erectus* first appeared in Africa about 1.7 million years ago. They have since spread to Asia, China, South-east Asia and parts of Europe. They are the first humans to travel out of Africa.

• Early humans have discovered how to make and control fire. They make hand-axes and scrapers from stones or flakes of rock for cutting meat, and fashion deer antlers and sticks of wood into tools and weapons.

> *The fire crackles and spits, and the smell of roasting meat wafts through the air. A group of humans—obviously human in their manner and actions, but still quite ape-like in appearance—busy themselves. The females tend to their young or collect firewood, while the males make tools or sit by the fire. They communicate with one another in a combination of sounds and gestures. Suddenly, a group of hyenas arrives on the scene, cackling murderously. They are driven off by humans wielding wooden clubs.*

NORTHERN CHINA

THE CONTINENT of North America will not be populated by humans for many thousands of years, but animals from distant parts of the world have made their way here. The mastodon, a type of elephant with extremely long tusks, has crossed the land bridge from Asia. Ground sloths like *Glossotherium* have come north from South America. All the animals are at risk from attack by sabre-toothed cats.

ELEPHANTS roam the forests of south-western France. Humans cannot hunt them, because their wooden spears are too flimsy to penetrate the thick hides of these huge animals. But sometimes an elephant will get stuck in a swamp and the humans can then finish it off. They could even drive it into such a trap by brandishing flaming torches. They use their stone scrapers to carve out the flesh.

MUCH OF northern Africa will one day be occupied by the dry wastes of the Sahara desert. At this time, however, it is a landscape of rolling grasslands and forests. The Nile flows through a lush environment inhabited by rhinos, hippos and lions. When the ice sheets return, this land will once more turn to desert, and the animals will migrate southwards.

GROUPS OF *Homo erectus* live in caves in northern China. *Homo erectus* have protruding jaws, thick brow ridges and low skulls. They are skilled toolmakers, and have learnt how to cook food over fires. Formidable hunters (they could probably communicate and make plans), they are still vulnerable to attack from other animals.

500,000 years ago

THE WORLD 35 million years ago

• This time in the Earth's history falls in the Oligocene Epoch. It marks a cooler phase in the Earth's climate following the continuous heatwave of the Eocene Epoch, during which forests covered both Poles.

• There is no grass. It will not appear for about another 15 million years.

• All the continents, except Europe and Asia, are separate from one another. Land mammals, which for the most part cannot cross the seas dividing continents, develop in different ways from one continent to another. (Somehow, though, monkeys find their away across from Africa to South America during this time.)

• The largest living animal on land is *Indricotherium (see opposite)*. It measures 13 feet high at the shoulder and weighs about 33,000 lbs.

• There are no humans on Earth, nor will there be for at least another 30 million years.

The air is alive with whooping and chattering noises. The great animals of the forest have come to the water's edge to drink, an event that always excites the birds and ape-like animals that live in the nearby trees. One of the new arrivals is elephant-like, but it has only a short trunk and four tusks, the lower two flat like a shovel. There are other animals that look just like rhinos from the side but, seen face-on, have two massive, cone-shaped horns—and two odd, knob-like projections—on their heads.

NILE VALLEY, EGYPT

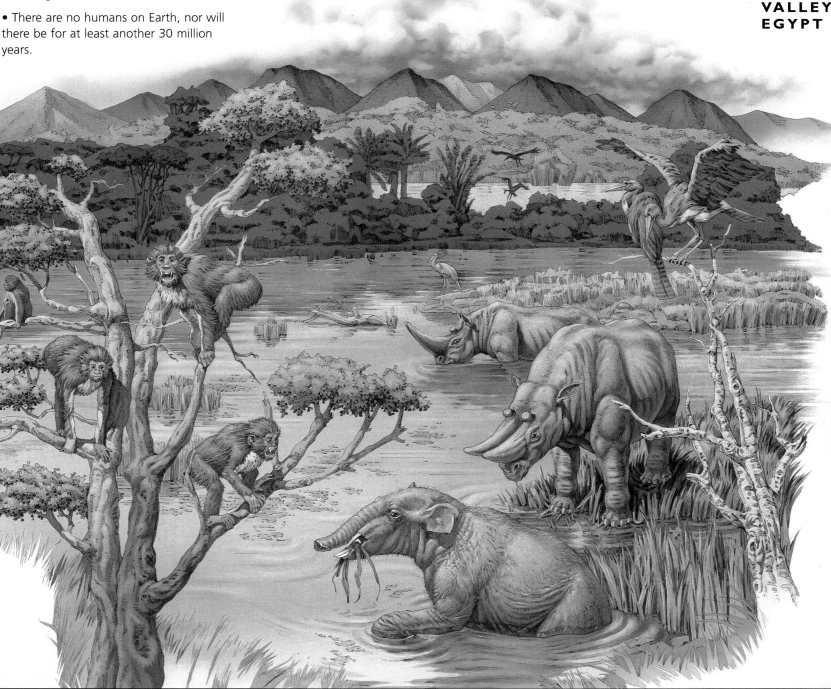

NEW YORK is a hot, swampy forest. Amazing animals like the ten feet tall *Brontops,* a member of a group of mammals called brontotheres, wallow in shallow waters, feeding on aquatic plants. These massive creatures have distinctive bony knobs on their snouts, which the males use to butt rivals for dominance. Meanwhile, in some more open parts of the forest, early horses called *Mesohippus* run free.

THIS PART of south-western France is covered by thick, humid forest. The climate is hot and wet. Various species of rhinoceros are common in Europe, including the hornless *Trigonias,* the earliest-known member of the rhinoceros family. Stalking it from the branches of an overhanging tree is the leopard-like *Nimravus,* one of the earliest cats. Bats and an opossum are other inhabitants of the night-time forest.

THE NILE flows through a tropical rainforest. Animals search for food in the swampy waters. They include the giant *Arsinoitherium,* similar to a two-horned rhinoceros, and *Phiomia,* a type of elephant. Overlooking the scene are ape-like animals climbing in the trees. These creatures are the first-known primates, the group of animals to which humans belong.

NORTHERN CHINA is a land of patchy trees and shrubs. Feeding off leaves growing in the highest branches is a huge member of the rhinoceros family, *Indricotherium.* Another giant leaf-eater, *Embolotherium,* has a strange bony structure on its head. Rooting about in the soil is *Archaeotherium,* an early kind of pig, which is being harried by two snarling *Hyaenodon.*

THE WORLD 80 million years ago

• This time in the Earth's history falls in the Cretaceous Period. Much of the world is covered by ocean or shallow seas. The area of land is only about half what it will be in modern times.

• India is an island. North America is split into two "islands", East and West. Antarctica is joined onto Australia. It is a warm continent, covered with forests and shrubs.

• At the end of the Cretaceous Period, some 15 million years later, about three-quarters of all living species, including all dinosaurs, will be wiped out.

• Dinosaurs are the only large land animals at this time. Reptiles dominate the skies and the seas, but there are also several species of birds and a number of different kinds of tiny mammals.

" Suddenly, a blood-chilling roar goes up. It is immediately answered by a series of booming, panicky hoots and the stamping of feet. A wild confusion ensues as a massive dinosaur launches itself at another, no less massive creature. With awesome power, the predator repeatedly tears at its victim's flesh with its dagger-like teeth. Meanwhile, another fight breaks out between a gang of smaller dinosaurs on the hunt and a pair of horned dinosaurs defending their nest. They exchange fierce, rasping cries. A horned dinosaur manages to butt one of its assailants to the ground. Two slender running dinosaurs flee the dangerous scene. "

NORTHERN CHINA

THE STIFLINGLY HOT, coastal flats make an ideal home for *Hadrosaurus*. Herds of these "duck-billed" dinosaurs (so-called because of their flat, beak-shaped mouths) roam the water's edge, pausing to forage for aquatic plants. They must be ever-watchful for giant, ferocious, meat-eating dinosaurs that may suddenly appear from nowhere to attack them. Tiny, shrew-like mammals will scurry around in the forest after dark.

SOUTH-WESTERN FRANCE, like much of southern Europe, lies under the sea. Only ancient mountaintops rise above the waves, forming small, rocky islets. Enormous plesiosaurs, marine reptiles with incredibly long, snake-like necks, swim close to the water's surface. Their heads dart this way and that as they snatch fish in their jaws. Sea birds and flying reptiles cruise overhead, watching for any leftovers.

THE NILE VALLEY is a wide expanse of slow-moving, brackish water. It is the domain of *Spinosaurus*. This carnivorous dinosaur wades through the shallow water, looking for fish. Quick as a flash, it hooks one out with its sharp thumb-claws and devours it. The sail on its back soaks up the sun's rays, enabling the animal to warm up quickly.

DINOSAURS thrive in the hot, dry climate of northern China. Flowering plants provide food for plant-eating species such as *Shantungosaurus* and the small, horned *Protoceratops*. These animals are, in turn, prey for the giant *Tarbosaurus* and such small, agile hunters as *Velociraptor*. Swooping above are giant pterosaurs the size of small aeroplanes.

THE WORLD 300 million years ago

• This time in the Earth's history falls in the Carboniferous Period. This period takes its name from the thick layers of coal (*carbo* is Latin for coal) that formed millions of years later from the vast, swampy, tropical forests of the age.

• The largest living things are trees: giant club mosses, *Lepidodendron,* grow as high as 130 feet. The largest animal may be *Eogyrinus,* a long-bodied amphibian (an animal that lives on land but breeds in water) about 16 feet long.

• Africa, South America, Australia, Antarctica and southern Asia are all joined together in the "supercontinent" of Gondwanaland. Drifting northwards, it is in the process of colliding with Laurasia, another supercontinent, made up of North America, Greenland, Europe and the rest of Asia.

• North America, Greenland and northern Europe all lie across the Equator.

It is extremely hot and humid. There are trees everywhere, many straight and tall, some fallen over. The ground is soft and boggy underfoot. Here and there, swampy waters, dense with rotting vegetation, have collected in stagnant pools. Insects—some the size of birds— zip to and fro, their beating wings humming noisily in the still air. Small animals scuttle along branches and under leaves. A gigantic centipede winds its way up a tree trunk, while a lizard-like creature stands motionless on a fallen tree trunk, ready to dart to safety. Several lumbering, almost dragon-like beasts drift through the swamp and heave themselves onto the ground, snorting menacingly.

NEW YORK is a dense, tropical, swampy forest. Insects flit among the tall trees and giant ferns, among them giant dragonflies with wingspans like those of seagulls. Amphibians wallow in the swampy waters. Millions of years before, some fish started to breathe air and walk on land using their fleshy fins. Some amphibians now live on land permanently: they are the first reptiles (one is seen here in the foreground).

SOUTH-WESTERN FRANCE lies under a shallow, tropical sea, rich in coral reefs and teeming with marine life. Starfish, sea urchins and ammonites drift among the coral, but fish, and sharks in particular, dominate the seas. Some kinds of shark look very strange indeed. There is one, *Stethacanthus,* that looks as if it has a brush attached to its back with the bristles—actually dozens of teeth—uppermost.

EGYPT lies in the southern hemisphere. Lush, swampy forests grow in the tropics in lands far to the north, while thick ice sheets are beginning to spread out from the South Pole in lands to the south. Here, between those two regions, there is arid desert. A few dry ferns grow amongst the rocks and sand, but there is no sign of the rich animal life of the forests.

NORTHERN CHINA, like parts of North America, Europe and Siberia, is a hot, flooded forest. Over millions of years, layer upon layer of plants and other living matter will decompose here, becoming compressed and eventually turning into coal seams sometimes hundreds of feet thick. (In this view on page 5, there is a coal mine.)

THE WORLD 550 million years ago

• This time in the Earth's history falls in the Cambrian Period. There has been a sudden increase in the variety of marine life-forms. No life exists on land.

• The continents lie in different positions to those of modern times. (Over millions of years, the continents will slowly drift around the globe.) Much of the land is flooded by shallow seas. North America lies in the tropics. Northern Europe and Siberia are located in the southern hemisphere.

• The great "supercontinent" of Gondwanaland dominates the southern hemisphere. Antarctica straddles the Equator, while west Africa lies near the South Pole.

• Living in the oceans are early forms of sponges, jellyfish and arthropods (animals with jointed legs and a body casing). There are no fish.

• The largest creature alive is probably *Anomalocaris* (pictured left centre), which is 2 feet long.

It's like something out of science fiction. There is a tiny beast with five mushroom-shaped eyes and a trunk with pincer-like jaws at the end of it. A big animal with a cloak-like body and two spiny graspers projecting forward from its head swims by. Edging slowly around the sea bed are some really amazing creatures. One is a scaly ball with spines sticking out all over. Another looks like a worm on seven pairs of stilts with a matching set of needle-like spines! Drifting through this weird menagerie is a pale, worm-like creature not so very different from a modern fish-like animal, the lancelet.

THE EARTH came into existence some 4600 million years ago. No one can say for sure how it happened, but many scientists agree on a likely sequence of events. The Solar System started life as a cloud of gas and dust drifting in space. Something, perhaps a shock wave from a star exploding nearby, caused the cloud to collapse under its own gravity. A huge, whirling disc was set in motion. Its center, where the force of gravity was strongest, became hotter and denser. This core of intense energy was the beginnings of our Sun. Dust fragments spinning around the center started to clump together, becoming first rocks, then boulders, and finally large, rocky bodies. One of these rocky bodies was the young Earth.

In its early days, Earth was a barren planet, continually bombarded by meteorites, rocky fragments crashing to the ground from space (**1**). These collisions caused the Earth's surface temperature to rise until the planet became a global sea of hot, molten rock (**2**). Eventually the surface cooled, but gases such as hydrogen, carbon dioxide, water vapour and nitrogen burst through the solid crust in volcanoes (**3**). These gases formed the Earth's atmosphere. Water vapour rose to form thick clouds. Rain began to fall, filling basins to form great oceans (**4**). Shallow, warm-water pools may have been the ideal environment for the formation of chemicals that would eventually become the building blocks of life.

ALL FOUR of our "windows" on the world, New York, south-western France, the Nile Valley and northern China, lie under water. The warm global climate has melted the polar ice caps, and the sea has encroached on many land masses. A scene like this might be found beneath the surface of any warm inland sea. There is a huge range of marine life forms—in contrast to the land, where there is no life at all. Some animals are anchored to the sea bed, while others creep through the mud or swim freely in the water. Living amongst the sponges and corals are some weird creatures quite unlike anything alive in modern times.

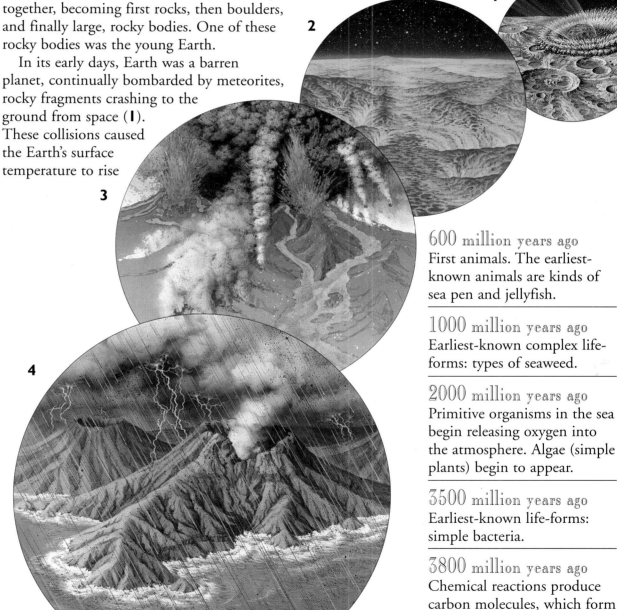

600 million years ago
First animals. The earliest-known animals are kinds of sea pen and jellyfish.

1000 million years ago
Earliest-known complex life-forms: types of seaweed.

2000 million years ago
Primitive organisms in the sea begin releasing oxygen into the atmosphere. Algae (simple plants) begin to appear.

3500 million years ago
Earliest-known life-forms: simple bacteria.

3800 million years ago
Chemical reactions produce carbon molecules, which form the basis for life.

4600 million years ago
The planet Earth is formed.

10 to 15 billion years ago

THE UNIVERSE comes into existence. The Universe consists of everything there is: galaxies, space, stars, planets and moons. All life-forms, including people, together with all objects, gases, liquids and so on, are part of the Universe. The birth of the Universe probably takes place in one colossal explosion called the Big Bang. During this explosion, all matter, energy, space—and time itself—are created. This moment can be truly described as the beginning of time, our journey's end.

From the moment the Universe comes into being, it takes another 100,000 years or so for atoms, the building blocks of matter, to form from their constituent parts: minute sub-atomic particles. Probably about 1 billion years later, gases clump together to form the first galaxies, enormous collections of stars. One of these galaxies (there are billions of them in the Universe) will be the birthplace of our own star, the Sun, around which Earth and all the other planets of the Solar System will form billions of years into the future.

INDEX

FURTHER READING LIST

Asimov, Isaac, *Our Planet Earth*. Gareth Stevens, 1995.

Brooks, Susan, *The Geography of the Earth*. New York: Oxford University Press, 1991.

Caselli, Giovanni, *The First Civilizations*. New York: Peter Bedrick Books, 1985.

Cotterell, Arthur, *Ancient China*. New York: Knopf Books for Young Readers, 1994.

Darling, Lois and Louis, *The Science of Life*. Cleveland and New York: The World Publishing Co., 1961.

Defrates, Joanna, *What Do We Know About the Egyptians?* New York: Peter Bedrick Books, 1992.

Dixon, Dougal, *The Search for Dinosaurs*. New York: Thomson Learning, 1995.

Eyewitness Books, *Early Humans*. New York: Alfred A. Knopf, 1989.

Fenton, Carroll Lane and Mildred Adams Fenton, *Prehistoric Zoo*. New York: Doubleday & Co. Inc., 1959.

Gregor, Arthur S., *Charles Darwin*. New York: E.P. Dutton & Co. Inc., 1966.

Lindsay, William, *Prehistoric Life*. New York: Alfred A. Knopf, 1994.

Morley, Jacqueline, *An Egyptian Pyramid*. New York: Peter Bedrick Books, 1991.

Pischel, Enrica C., *China from the 10th to 19th Century*. Raintree-Steck-Vaughn, 1994.

Simon, Seymour, *Our Solar System*. New York: Morrow Junior Books, 1992.

Skelton, Renee, *Charles Darwin and the Theory of Natural Selection*. New York: Barron's, 1987.

The British Museum, *Dinosaurs and their Living Relatives*. New York: Cambridge University Press, 1979, 1985.

White, Jon Manchip, *Everyday Life in Ancient Egypt*. New York: G.P. Putnam's Sons, 1963. Reprinted Dorset Books, NY and Peter Bedrick Books, NY.

ADVANCED READING LIST

Cunliffe, Barry, ed., *Origins: The Roots of European Civilization*. London: BBC Books, 1981.

Kurtén, Björn, *Our Earliest Ancestors*. New York: Columbia University Press, 1993.

Leakey, Richard A. and Roger Lewin, *Origins*. New York: E.P. Dutton, 1997.

Lovelock, James, *The Ages of Gaia: A Biography of Our Living Earth*. New York: W.W. Norton & Co. Inc., 1988, 1995.

Muschie, Guy, *The Seven Mysteries of Life*. Boston: Houghton Mifflin Co., 1978.

Redfield, Robert, *The Primitive World and Its Transformations*. Ithaca, New York: Cornell University Press, 1953.

Sagan, Carl, *Cosmos*. New York: Random House, 1980.

Vlahos, Olivia, *Human Beginnings*. New York: The Viking Press, 1966.